Free your creativity

How to stimulate your innovation and turn your
ideas into reality

Jane Hawkins

SUMMARY

CHAPTER 1: INTRODUCTION

Ideas are the fuel of human innovation and creativity.

For millennia, human beings have been encouraged to think, invent and explore their own abilities.

However, it can be difficult to unleash your creativity and turn your ideas into reality.

That's where stimulating your innovation comes in.

Innovation stimulation is a process of stimulating your mind to generate innovative ideas and implement creative solutions to problems.

It is an active and dynamic process that can have positive effects on your ability to create and innovate.

In this chapter, we will explore ways to stimulate your innovation and turn your ideas into reality.

We'll look at strategies to stimulate your creativity, ways to develop your innovation, and tools that can help you turn your ideas into reality.

<u>Stimulating your creativity</u>

Stimulating your creativity is the first step to unleashing your innovation.

There are many ways to stimulate your creativity, including:

- Take time to think.

Taking time to reflect on your ideas and problems can help develop new perspectives and boost your creativity.

- Listen.

Listening to others can help you stimulate your imagination and discover interesting and innovative ideas.

- Learn something new.

Learning a new skill or subject can help you stimulate your creativity.

- Interact with your peers.

Sharing your ideas and problems with your peers can help you boost your creativity and develop new solutions.
- Take breaks.

Taking breaks allows your mind to rest and think of new ideas.

- Find creative ways to solve problems.

Finding creative ways to solve common problems can help you boost your creativity and develop new ideas.

<u>Develop your innovation</u>

Once you have stimulated your creativity, you need to develop your innovation.

There are many ways to develop your innovation, including:

- Develop a vision.

Developing a clear and consistent vision of your goal will help you drive your innovation and focus on the process of implementing your ideas.

- Learn from your mistakes.

Learning from your mistakes is a great way to develop your innovation and find innovative solutions to problems.
- Seek information.

Seeking information about innovative ideas and solutions to common problems can help you develop your innovation.

- Test your ideas.

Testing your ideas can help you develop and improve your ideas and find innovative and effective solutions to problems.

- Develop a strategy.

Developing a clear and consistent strategy for implementing your ideas can help you develop your innovation and achieve your goals.

<u>Tools to turn your ideas into reality</u>

Once you have developed your innovation and have a clear vision of your goal, you need to find tools to turn your ideas into reality.

There are many tools and resources that can help you turn your ideas into reality, including:

- Prototyping.

Prototyping allows you to test and develop your ideas by creating models and simulations.

- Data modeling.

Data modeling can help you collect and analyze data to make better decisions and implement innovative solutions.

- Collaboration tools.

Collaboration tools can help you work in teams and foster collaboration and innovation.

- Project management tools.

Project management tools can help you organize and manage your project effectively and achieve your goals.

Conclusion

Stimulating innovation and creativity is the surest way to turn your ideas into reality.

The key steps to unleashing your innovation are stimulating your creativity, developing your innovation and finding ways to turn your ideas into reality.

There are many tools and resources that can help you unlock your creativity and turn your ideas into reality.

CHAPTER 2: DISCOVER YOUR CREATIVITY

Have you ever wondered what creativity is?

And how you can develop it?

Creativity is actually a process that is unique to each of us and allows us to find innovative solutions to the problems we face.

In this chapter, we will explore how you can discover your own creativity and use it to advance your work and your life.

First, we must remember that we are all endowed with creative potential.

There is no difference between those who are considered "creative" and those who are not.

Everyone has the ability to think creatively and find innovative solutions.

However, this creative potential can only be developed if we nurture and stimulate it.

For this, it is important to understand how the creative process works.

It starts with awareness and understanding of your environment.

You need to take the time to look around and immerse yourself in different situations that can give you different perspectives.

Once you are aware of your surroundings, you can begin to focus on identifying and exploring possibilities.

You can also stimulate your imagination by asking yourself questions about what is possible and what is not.

This will give you a sense of what you can create.

Once you have a good understanding of what is possible, you can begin to explore more concrete ideas.

You can focus on finding solutions to specific problems and you can use brainstorming techniques or exploration methods to help you come up with innovative ideas.

Finally, you need to keep your focus on implementing your ideas.

You can do this by thinking about the different ways you could implement them and weighing the pros and cons of each option.

You can also make connections between your ideas and those of others to see if more innovative solutions can be found.

Finally, you can start implementing your ideas by testing them and adjusting them based on the results.

In summary, discovering and unleashing your creativity is essential to developing innovative solutions.

To do this, you must take the time to understand your environment, explore possibilities, identify ideas and implement your solutions.

If you do this, you will be able to find innovative solutions and boost your innovation.

CHAPTER 3: LEARN TO LISTEN TO YOURSELF

As creative beings, we all have moments of doubt and confusion.

It is normal to feel overwhelmed at times by the magnitude of our projects and not know how to move forward.

Learning to listen to yourself can be an effective way to find solutions to these moments and to develop your creativity.

One of the first steps in learning to listen to yourself is to develop your ability to focus.

Concentration helps us to open up to our thoughts and emotions without being distracted by surrounding noise and distractions.

Once we have found inner silence, we can begin to listen to our mind and discover what it has to tell us.

Once we are calm and have found inner silence, we can move into the practice of meditation.

Meditation is a great way to start focusing and listening to ourselves.

Meditation allows us to connect with our thoughts and emotions, which allows us to step back and better understand what is going on inside of us.

Another way to connect with yourself is to start noticing your reactions and feelings.

By becoming aware of how you feel, you can better understand what motivates you and what inspires you.

For example, if you notice that you feel overwhelmed by a project, you can step back and understand what scares you.

Once you are aware of your emotions, you can begin to explore them more deeply.

Take the time to ask yourself questions and look for answers.

For example, what scares you?

What is holding you back?

What changes can you make to your project that will make you feel more comfortable and capable of completing it?

Learning to listen to yourself is an important step in the creative process.

By taking the time to examine your thoughts and emotions, you can better understand what motivates and inspires you and thus find more effective solutions.

Finally, once you have taken the time to listen to yourself, you can begin to apply the lessons you have learned.

Take the time to put the solutions into practice and start seeing results.

That's when you'll start to see your ideas turn into reality.

In conclusion, learning to listen to yourself is an important step in developing your creativity and learning to turn your ideas into reality.

By taking the time to open up to your thoughts and emotions, you will be better able to understand what motivates you and what inspires you.

Once you've found solutions, you can put what you've learned into practice and start seeing results.

CHAPTER 4: FIND YOUR INSPIRATION

You may have heard the words "find your inspiration" before, but not know how to go about it.

In fact, finding inspiration can be a pretty tricky and personal process, and it requires some discipline and a good dose of creativity.

In this chapter, we'll show you how to find your inspiration and how you can use it to boost your creativity and turn your ideas into reality.

First, it is important to understand what inspiration is.

Inspiration is the spark of genius that drives someone to make a decision or create something.

It is a spark that gives you the energy and motivation to achieve your goals.

It can come from anywhere, from books and movies to conversations and personal experiences.

Regardless of its source, inspiration can help you develop new ideas, find creative solutions to problems and stimulate your creativity.

Once you understand what inspiration is and why it's so important, it's time to get practical.

Here are some tips for finding your inspiration:

1. Take time for yourself.

The first step to finding your inspiration is to take time for yourself.

Get away from noise and distractions and spend time thinking about what is important to you and what inspires you.

You could listen to music, read a book, take a walk or even just sit and meditate.

2. Find your creative space.

Once you have found what inspires you, you need to find a place to focus and release your creativity.

This can be a place in your home, a park or a coffee shop.

Find the perfect place for you and dedicate time to working in that space each day.

3. Explore new horizons.

One way to find your inspiration is to get out of your comfort zone and explore new horizons.

Visit different places, meet different people and learn new things.

You'll be surprised at all the ideas that will emerge from this exploration.

4. Record your ideas.

Once you have found your inspiration, you need to use it to turn your ideas into reality.

To do this, you need to record your ideas as soon as you have them and analyze them later.

You can do this on a piece of paper, a notebook or a laptop.

5. Don't compare yourself to others.

A common mistake many people make is to compare themselves to others.

Don't be intimidated by what others are doing and don't let it distract you from your own path.

Remember that your creativity is unique and only you can develop it.

6. Don't get distracted.

Another common mistake people make is to get distracted. Don't let social media, television or radio distract you from your work.

Find a way to focus on your project and what really matters.

By using these tips, you can find your source of inspiration and you can use it to spark your creativity and turn your ideas into reality.

Remember, the process is personal and you need to find ways to get inspired that work for you.

Take the time to find what inspires you and unleash your creativity.

CHAPTER 5: EVALUATE AND DEVELOP YOUR IDEAS

When you are faced with a particular problem or situation, you need to take time to think and brainstorm solutions and ideas.

This is where evaluating and developing your ideas comes in.

Evaluation and development of your ideas allows you to determine whether or not your idea is feasible and what actions need to be taken to make it happen.

This is a critical process that helps you make more informed decisions and turn your ideas into reality.

First, you need to have a clear understanding of the ideas you have generated.

It is important to take the time to carefully review them and evaluate them for their potential.

To do this, you can ask questions such as:

"What are the pros and cons of this idea?"

"Is this idea feasible?"

"What are the obstacles I will have to overcome to implement it?"

Once you have evaluated your ideas, you need to develop and refine them.

You can start by writing a detailed plan of what you need to do to make it happen.

This can include research, solution development, resources needed, and steps to follow.

Next, you can create a timeline and budget to help you achieve your goals.

Another way to develop your ideas is to test them.

You can test your ideas by submitting them to experts and peers for feedback and suggestions.

You can also use tools such as surveys, questionnaires, and interviews to gather information and insights about your ideas.

Once you have evaluated and developed your ideas, you are ready to implement them.

You need to review your plans again and clarify the steps needed to implement them.

You may need to find partners, investors and funding sources to help you realize your project.

You will also need to take steps to ensure that your project complies with applicable laws and regulations.

In summary, evaluating and developing your ideas is essential to help you make more informed decisions and turn your ideas into reality.

It is important to take the time to understand your ideas and develop them to their potential.

You will also need to test your ideas and prepare plans to implement them.

Finally, you will need to take steps to ensure that your project complies with applicable laws and regulations.

CHAPTER 6: USING TECHNOLOGY TO HELP YOU

In our modern world, technology is everywhere. We use it to communicate, work, learn, entertain and even for innovation.

Technology can be a great tool to help you unleash your creativity and turn your ideas into reality.

First of all, technology can help you come up with new ideas.

Many companies use online platforms to develop ideas and gather feedback on the products and services they offer.

These platforms give users the ability to share their ideas and vote for others' ideas.

These platforms also give companies the opportunity to collect feedback on their products and services and use this information to improve their products and services.

In addition, the internet and social networks can help you find inspiration and connect with others who share the same ideas and interests.

You can find online communities of people who share ideas and knowledge, and you can also find people to contact to discuss your ideas.

In addition, you can find groups and forums that are dedicated to specific topics and common interests to help you develop ideas.

Next, technology can help you turn your ideas into reality.

Computer tools such as design, planning and development software can help you create and implement your ideas.

In addition, there are digital tools such as visualization software, databases, and analysis tools that can help you organize and evaluate your ideas.

Finally, you can use technology to promote and market your products and services, and to communicate with your customers.

In addition, technology can help you better understand the ideas of others and develop relationships.

Online tools and platforms can facilitate collaboration and idea sharing among team members.

You can also use digital tools such as analytics and visualization tools to better understand others' ideas and help you improve them.

Finally, technology can help you find solutions to your problems.

You can use computer tools to solve complex problems and come up with innovative and creative solutions.

You can also use digital tools to collect and analyze data to make more informed decisions.

In conclusion, technology can help you unleash your creativity and turn your ideas into reality.

Use technology to come up with new ideas, to better understand the ideas of others, and to find solutions to your problems.

Use technology to help you develop your ideas and turn them into reality.

CHAPTER 7: USING BRAINSTORMING

The brainstorming method is a very effective technique to develop new ideas and find innovative solutions.

The goal is to stimulate a group or an individual to come up with innovative and creative ideas.

This method can be used to solve problems, develop products or services, innovate and find alternatives.

Brainstorming begins with a group of collaborators gathered around a table.

Participants should be invited to express themselves freely and share their thoughts.

Each member of the group should be encouraged to share his or her ideas and to contribute to improving the ideas of others.

The first step is to define the purpose and topic of the brainstorming.

The purpose may be to find solutions to a specific problem, to develop a product or service, or to innovate.

Once the topic is defined, it is important to clarify the different concepts and their limits.

The second step is to stimulate the creativity of the participants.

It is important to create a relaxed environment.

Participants should be encouraged to share their ideas and be open to exploring alternatives.

It is also important to remind participants that all ideas are good ideas and that all suggestions should be considered.

Once ideas have been shared, the group can begin to develop them.

Participants can focus on one idea at a time and discuss it in depth.

This step is very important for developing more complete ideas and more innovative solutions.

The third step is to select the best ideas and evaluate them.

Participants can agree on which ideas are the most promising and useful.

Selecting the best ideas may require debate and discussion.

It is important to let all participants speak and listen to their views.
The fourth step is to implement the selected ideas.

Once the best ideas have been identified, it is time to put them into action.

Participants must agree on a plan of action and define the steps to follow to reach their goal.

Brainstorming is a very effective method to stimulate creativity and encourage innovation.

This method can be used to solve problems, develop new products and services, and find innovative solutions.

Brainstorming can provide very satisfying results when it is well managed.

It is important to remember that brainstorming can be a long and difficult process, but the results can be very rewarding.

CHAPTER 8: DEVELOPING YOUR NETWORK

When undertaking an innovative project, developing your network can be the key to success.

The relationships you have with those around you can provide you with resources, advice and information that will help you achieve your goals.

But how do you develop your network and leverage it to support your innovation?

First, you can start by surrounding yourself with the right people.

People who have the same interests as you, who are involved in the same industry as you or who are more experienced than you.

These people can give you advice and encourage you to pursue your plans.

You can find these people online or at conferences, seminars or trade shows.

You can also go to associations or groups that can help you connect and grow your network.

Once you have found people who share your interests, you need to keep in touch.

You can do this by sending them emails from time to time and inviting them to events.

You can also follow them on social networks and participate in online conversations with them.

You can also ask people to help you develop your network.

The people you connect with can introduce you to others who might be helpful.

You can also ask them to share your ideas and products with their friends and contacts.

Once you have developed your network, you need to maintain it.

You need to be in touch with your contacts and show them that you are available to help them.

You can send them updates on your projects and ask for their feedback and help.

You can also offer them collaborations and partnerships.

Finally, you can use your network to find funding and support for your project.

You can ask your contacts to help you find investors or sponsors.

You can also ask them to recommend you to companies that might be interested in your product or service.

Developing and maintaining a network can be critical to the success of your innovation.

It can help you find information, advice and resources to make your project happen.

It can also help you find funding and support to make it happen.

So start developing your network and use it to drive your innovation and turn your ideas into reality.

CHAPTER 9: DEVELOPING YOUR DISCIPLINE

Developing your discipline is one of the key elements that will help you unleash your creativity and stimulate your innovation.

It is a process that allows you to develop a positive attitude and planning and time management skills that will allow you to achieve your goals effectively and efficiently.

Discipline is a quality that can be developed, and it starts with a strong willingness to put in the work and commit to the goals you have set for yourself.

Disciplined also means being able to make tough decisions and stick to them, even if those decisions are not always popular.

Finally, being disciplined means being able to manage your emotions and thoughts so that you can make rational and constructive decisions.

To develop your discipline, you must first define your short- and long-term goals and commit to achieving them.

You also need to develop a routine and schedule to ensure that you stay focused and achieve your goals.

Once you have defined your goals and established a routine, you need to learn how to manage your time effectively.

It is important to know how to prioritize and organize your tasks so that you can do the important tasks first and the less important tasks last.

You also need to learn how to say no to distractions and be disciplined so that you don't get distracted by things that aren't related to your goals.

Another way to develop your discipline is to set rules and boundaries for yourself.

You need to learn to discipline yourself and challenge yourself to make sure that you are following the rules and boundaries that you have set for yourself.

You also need to learn to accept the fact that you can't do everything and accept that sometimes you have to make tough decisions to achieve your goals.

Another way to develop your discipline is to surround yourself with people who share the same goals as you.

These people will help encourage you and keep you on track to achieve your goals.

They will also help you remember that you can do it and stay motivated when things get tough.

Finally, you need to be prepared for the failures and difficulties that may arise on your way to success.

It is important to know that failures and obstacles are part of the process and that you must learn from your mistakes and continue to improve.

By developing your discipline, you will be able to unleash your creativity and stimulate your innovation.

You will be able to turn your ideas into reality and make them happen.

You will be able to manage your time effectively and commit to your goals.

You will be able to make tough decisions and discipline yourself to achieve your goals.

Finally, you will be able to surround yourself with people who share the same goals as you and be prepared to deal with the failures and difficulties that will arise.

CHAPTER 10: USING TIME MANAGEMENT TOOLS

Introduction

Using time management tools is a way to increase your productivity and unleash your creativity.

Time management tools can help you plan, organize and prioritize your tasks and get more time to focus on your ideas and creativity.

In this chapter, you will learn how to leverage time management tools to gain productivity and free up more time for your creative projects.

We'll look at the different time management tools available and how to use them so that you can find the one that works best for you.

We will also discuss methods to help you manage your time more effectively and free up time for your creative ideas.

We'll also look at the pros and cons of time management tools, and explain how to use them to help you achieve your goals and turn your ideas into reality.

What is time management?

Time management is a method of organizing your activities and planning your tasks in order to better manage your time and gain productivity.

Time management is an effective solution to optimize your time and to help you reach your goals faster and more efficiently.

Today, there are many time management tools that allow you to better organize your tasks, prioritize your activities and find more time for your creative projects.

These tools can help you save time and better manage your time to achieve your goals.

<u>The benefits of time management</u>

Time management can help you manage your time better and be more productive.

By planning and organizing your tasks, you can save time and focus on your goals.

Time management can also help you better prioritize your activities and find more time for your creative ideas.

Time management can also help you reduce stress, feel calmer and be more productive.

By planning and organizing your activities, you can gain efficiency and time, which will help you have more time and energy for your creative projects.

<u>Time management tools</u>

There are many time management tools available to help you better manage your time.

These tools can help you plan, organize and prioritize your tasks and find more time for your creative projects.

Time management tools can be divided into four categories: planning tools, task management tools, attention management tools and productivity measurement tools.

Planning tools help you plan and organize your activities and prioritize your tasks.

They can also help you find more time for your creative projects and manage your time better.

Task management tools help you manage and organize your activities and find more time for your creative projects.

They can also help you better prioritize your tasks and find more time for your creative projects.

Attention management tools help you stay focused and on task.
They can help you avoid distractions and find more time for your creative projects.

Productivity measurement tools help you measure and evaluate your productivity and find ways to be more productive.

They can also help you find more time for your creative projects and manage your time better.

How to use time management tools

When using time management tools, it's important to remember that the tools won't help you save time if you don't know how to use them properly.

It is important to take the time to understand the tools and use them appropriately to get the best results.

Before you start using time management tools, you need to take the time to define your goals and plan your tasks.

You should also take the time to determine which time management tool is right for you and configure it to meet your needs and goals.

Once you have defined your goals and chosen a time management tool, you need to take the time to use it properly.

You need to make sure that you plan your tasks and prioritize your activities so that you can better manage your time and find more time for your creative projects.

You also need to make sure you measure and evaluate your productivity so you can find ways to become more productive.

You can use productivity measurement tools to measure and evaluate your productivity and find ways to be more productive and find more time for your creative projects.

<u>Conclusion</u>

Time management is an effective way to optimize your time and help you achieve your goals faster and more efficiently.

There are many time management tools that can help you plan, organize and prioritize your tasks and find more time for your creative projects.

You need to take the time to define your goals and plan your tasks, as well as choose and set up the time management tool that works best for you.

You also need to take the time to use these tools well and to measure and evaluate your productivity so you can find ways to be more productive and find more time for your creative projects.

By applying the principles of time management and using the tools at your disposal, you can save time and free up time for your creative projects to drive your innovation and turn your ideas into reality.

CHAPTER 11: LEARN TO WORK AS A TEAM

Innovations and ideas are meaningless if they are not put into practice.

To turn your ideas into reality, you must learn to work as a team.

A team succeeds when each member builds on the strengths and skills of others to achieve a common goal.

Learning to work in teams is essential to fostering creativity and collaboration.

First, to learn how to work in a team, you must understand the role of each team member and recognize what makes them unique.

Each member makes a unique contribution to the team and should be recognized for that.

Once you understand the role of each team member, you must learn to work in synergy with them to achieve a common goal.

To learn how to work as a team, you must ensure that all team members understand their roles and responsibilities.

You also need to make sure that everyone is aware of the team's goals and how they can contribute to achieving them.

Each team member must be aware of the other members and their skills in order to work together effectively.

Once you understand each member's role and responsibilities, you must learn to communicate and collaborate constructively.

To do this, you must create a positive and supportive work environment.

This means listening to and encouraging the contributions of other team members.

You also need to ensure that team members are comfortable speaking freely and without fear.

Once you have created a positive and constructive work environment, you must learn to coordinate the team's efforts.

You need to make sure the team is working together and that everyone is doing their part.

You also need to make sure that the work is done on time and that the goals are met.

Finally, to learn to work as a team, you must learn to accept and incorporate feedback.

Feedback is important because it allows you to improve the team's work and help you achieve your goals.

You must be open to criticism and suggestions from other team members.

In summary, learning to work as a team is essential to foster creativity and collaboration.

You must understand the role and responsibilities of each team member and learn to communicate and collaborate constructively.

You must also learn to coordinate team efforts and to accept and incorporate feedback.

If you apply these principles, you will be able to turn your ideas into reality.

CHAPTER 12: BUILDING YOUR CONFIDENCE

Creative people need strong self-confidence to succeed.

Self-confidence is essential for moving forward and finding ways to deal with life's challenges and obstacles.

Self-confidence can be developed and strengthened through certain strategies and techniques that can be applied on a daily basis.

The first step in developing self-confidence is to accept your imperfections.

No one is perfect and everyone has flaws.

However, these imperfections are what make us unique and give us a special personality.

It is therefore important to accept and embrace them instead of rejecting them.

Second, it's important to focus on what you're good at.

It's easy to feel discouraged when faced with complex tasks, but focusing on what you already know how to do, and trying to learn new skills, can build your confidence.

The third tip is to find a mentor or role model who can show you how to succeed and who can help you achieve your goals.

You can also find a support group of people who have the same goals as you.

These people can encourage you and help you stay motivated.

Another way to build self-confidence is to set short-term and long-term goals and challenges.

Small, short-term goals can offer a sense of accomplishment and can help build confidence.

Long-term goals can help give your life a broader meaning and help you learn and grow.

It is important to set boundaries and know how to say no to others and yourself.

It's easy to feel overwhelmed and exhausted trying to accomplish too much at once.

Learning to say no and set boundaries can help you feel more confident in your ability to handle responsibilities and tasks.

Finally, it's important to take time to relax and reflect.

Taking time to reflect and ask questions about your life can help you gain a better understanding of yourself and build your confidence.

Taking time to do things you enjoy as well can help build your confidence.

With these tips and techniques, you can build your confidence and feel more comfortable with yourself.

Self-confidence is an essential skill for creative and innovative people, and by developing your self-confidence, you can reach your goals and full creative potential.

CHAPTER 13: CULTIVATE YOUR CREATIVITY

Creativity is a fundamental element of human life.

It allows people to express themselves freely, to create works of art, to develop innovative products or services and to find solutions to complex problems.

Without creativity, the world would be a much duller and boring place.

However, creativity is not innate in everyone. It must be cultivated and nurtured to be fully utilized.

In this chapter, we will examine what it means to cultivate creativity and how to do it.

First, we will look at what it means to cultivate creativity.

Cultivating creativity means taking the time to think creatively and explore ideas and approaches that are new and different.

It also means giving yourself the opportunity to explore and be wrong.

Creativity is the product of exploration and risk-taking.

By taking the time to cultivate creativity, you give yourself the opportunity to develop innovative ideas and solutions.

Once we understand what it means to cultivate creativity, we can move on to the question of how to do it.

There are many ways to cultivate your creativity, but here are some of the most important.

First, develop your creative skills.

Creative skills are skills that help you generate ideas, evaluate them, and turn them into concrete solutions.

These skills can be developed by taking classes, reading books or working with mentors.

Second, take time to relax and reflect.

Relaxation and reflection are essential to cultivating creativity.

Take time to sit and think about problems and possible solutions.

You can also relax by doing creative activities, such as music, drawing or crafts.

Third, explore new areas and learn new things.

Exploration is one of the keys to developing creativity.

If you explore new areas, you can develop new ideas and find innovative solutions to problems.

Learn new things and discover new ways to solve problems.

Fourth, surround yourself with creative and inspiring people.

Creativity is contagious and you can benefit by surrounding your life with creative people.

These people can help you develop new ideas and find new solutions to problems.

Finally, cultivate your passion.

Passion is an essential part of creativity.

If you are passionate about a topic or area, you will be more motivated to find innovative solutions to problems and develop ideas.

In short, cultivating your creativity means taking the time to think creatively and explore ideas and approaches that are new and different.

To cultivate your creativity, you need to develop your creative skills, take time to relax and reflect, explore new areas and learn new things, surround yourself with creative and inspiring people and cultivate your passion.

By following these tips, you can develop your creativity and boost your innovation.

CHAPTER 14: TAKE BREAKS

When you are looking for inspiration and innovative ideas, it is important to take regular breaks.

Breaks can help you relax, focus and think of new ideas.

In this chapter, we'll explain how to take breaks and give you practical tips to stimulate your creativity and turn your ideas into reality.

Breaks are important because they allow us to step back and think about new perspectives.

By taking a break, you can step back from your work and give yourself time to let your mind wander.

When you take a break, you can focus on your goals and allow yourself to be more creative.

Breaks can also help us reconnect with what is important to us.

A break can give us the opportunity to take a moment to focus on our values, goals and dreams.

Taking time to reflect on these things allows us to focus on what we really want to achieve.

Breaks can also help us better understand our work and find solutions to difficult problems.

A break can give us time to step back and analyze a problem more deeply.

It can help us find innovative and creative solutions to our problems.

But how do you take breaks effectively?

First, you should take the time to plan your breaks.

Planning your day can help you organize your breaks and find the right time to take them.

You can also plan longer breaks, such as a lunch break or a weekend break.

Then you should make sure you take regular breaks.

Breaks can help us relax and think of new ideas.

And, by taking more frequent breaks, you can ensure that you are always thinking of new perspectives and stimulating your creativity.

Once you take a break, you should focus on what you can learn and how you can apply what you've learned to your work.

You can take time to think about questions such as:

How might I approach this problem differently?

What new perspectives can I find?

What can I learn from this experience?

You should also make sure to take regular breaks to relax and have fun.
You could take a walk, play a video game, watch a movie or listen to music.

These activities can help you relax and stimulate your creative mind.
Finally, you should make sure to take regular breaks and make time for yourself.

Taking breaks to take care of your physical and mental health is an important part of boosting your creativity and turning your ideas into reality.

Taking time to relax and do activities that give you pleasure can help you come up with innovative solutions and new ideas.

In conclusion, breaks are important to stimulate your creativity and turn your ideas into reality.

By taking regular breaks and focusing on what you can learn and how you can apply what you have learned to your work, you can stimulate your creative mind and come up with innovative solutions to your problems.

Don't forget to take time to relax and have fun to ensure you are always thinking of new perspectives and stimulating your creativity.

CHAPTER 15: USING THE VISUALIZATION

In this chapter, we'll explore how visualization can help you unleash your creativity and boost your innovation.

We'll look at how to use visualization to better understand and explore ideas, as well as simple techniques for integrating visualization into your creative process.

Visualization is an art form and a way of thinking that allows us to see and understand things differently.

It is a powerful method for communicating ideas, concepts and information.

Visualization allows you to see ideas and concepts that are not visible to the naked eye.

Visualization can be used to explore and experiment with ideas and concepts.

Using images, colors, shapes and words, you can create visual representations of your thoughts and ideas.

This allows you to develop new perspectives and explore solutions more deeply.

One of the main ways to use visualization is to create concept maps.

A concept map is a graphic representation that shows how ideas and concepts are related to each other.

Concept maps can be created using words, phrases, colors, and symbols, and can be used to explore and experiment with ideas and concepts.

Another way to use visualization is the "six hats" method.

This method is based on the idea of thinking about a problem or idea from different perspectives.

It is based on the principle that you can see things from different angles and approach problems from different viewpoints.

This method can be useful for exploring ideas and solutions.

You can imagine wearing different "hats" and exploring the problem from different perspectives.

This allows you to explore new ideas and perspectives.

There are also visualization techniques that can be used to explore ideas and solutions.

For example, you can use mental images, imaginary scenes and colors to develop concepts and ideas.

You can also use diagrams, drawings and charts to communicate information and concepts.

Finally, you can also use models and simulations to experiment with solutions and test ideas.

These models and simulations can help you understand how your solution will work and how it can be improved.

In short, visualization can be a powerful tool to unleash your creativity and drive innovation.

By using simple techniques such as mind maps, the six-hat method, and mental images, you can explore new ideas and perspectives.

You can also use models and simulations to experiment with solutions and test ideas.

Finally, you can use diagrams, drawings and charts to communicate information and concepts.

By using visualization, you can develop new perspectives and turn your ideas into reality.

CHAPTER 16: WORKING OUTSIDE YOUR COMFORT ZONE

Working outside your comfort zone can be a rewarding experience and a source of creativity and innovation.

It is a way to open yourself up to new perspectives, new challenges and new opportunities.

The comfort zone is a mental and physical state that allows us to feel comfortable and safe.

It is the place where we feel most comfortable and relaxed because we know what we are doing and feel in control of the situation.

When we step out of our comfort zone, we are faced with challenges, uncertainties and risks that push us to step out of our routine and find new solutions.

Working outside of your comfort zone can be both a scary and exhilarating process.

It's important to understand that it's normal to feel anxious and nervous when doing something new and that it's part of the process.

This is how we grow and improve.

The important thing is to focus on the benefits it can bring and find ways to overcome the stress and anxiety.

One way to start working outside of your comfort zone is to set short-term and long-term goals.

Short-term goals are goals that are easier to achieve and can help you feel comfortable in a new environment.

Long-term goals are more challenging and can help you move out of your comfort zone and grow.

It can also help you assess your progress and motivate you to keep improving.

Another way to work outside your comfort zone is to find people who can encourage and support you.

These people can be friends, colleagues, or mentors who are willing to help you get out of your comfort zone and support you in your development.

Finding supportive and encouraging people can be a great way to feel more comfortable and confident in a new situation.

Another way to get out of your comfort zone is to take risks.

Taking risks may seem scary, but it's an important part of the innovation and creativity process.

Risks can help you get out of your comfort zone and come up with new ideas and solutions.

When taking risks, it's important to make sure you're willing to take the consequences.

This can be a way to learn and improve.

Finally, the last way to work outside of your comfort zone is to take time to reflect on your goals and aspirations.

Taking the time to think about what you want to accomplish and how you are going to get there can be a very helpful way to get out of your comfort zone and boost your creativity and innovation.

Taking time to think about your goals can help you clarify your ideas and find new ways to achieve them.

Working outside of your comfort zone can be a very rewarding and challenging way to improve your creativity and innovation.

It's important to understand that this can be a time-consuming and challenging process.

However, by taking the time to think about your goals and aspirations and finding people who can support and encourage you, you can find new ways to step outside your comfort zone and boost your creativity and innovation.

CHAPTER 17: LISTEN TO YOUR INSTINCTS

When faced with challenges and problems, you've probably heard that you should listen to your instincts.

But what does that really mean?

And how can you learn to listen to and trust your instincts?

In this chapter, we'll explore these questions and teach you how to develop your intuition and listen to your gut to be more creative and innovative.

First, what is instinct?

Instinct is a form of intuition that comes from feelings and emotions deep within your being.

It is more than just a hunch or a guess, it is a feeling or sensation that is rooted in your body and tells you what to do or not to do in a certain situation.

Instinct is a form of intelligence that is rooted in your being and allows you to make decisions faster, more efficiently and with more confidence.

Instinct is a powerful tool that can help you be more creative and innovative.

However, it is important to understand that your instinct will not always tell you the perfect solution.

It may give you clues as to where to go, but the process of making decisions and solving problems remains your responsibility.

So how do you listen to your gut?

The first step is to learn to identify your feelings and emotions.

Become aware of what you feel and how you feel when you are faced with a difficult situation or dilemma.

Once you have identified what you are feeling, you can begin to listen to and trust your instincts.

Another way to listen to your instincts is to practice meditation and relaxation.

Meditation and relaxation help you refocus and reconnect to your inner self.

By relaxing and focusing on your body sensations, you can begin to listen to the whisper of your gut and trust its guidance.

Another way to listen to your gut is to take time to reflect and step back.

Take time to understand the different aspects of a problem and consider the different options available to you.

Once you have taken the time to reflect on the situation, you can then listen to your gut and make a decision that is best for you.

Finally, in order to listen to your instincts, you must learn to trust your intuition.

Your intuition offers you insights and perspectives that are often deeper and more valuable than what your mind can offer.

Learn to listen to and trust your intuition and gut and you will find that you are able to make decisions faster and with more confidence.

By listening to and trusting your instincts, you will be able to understand problems better and make more creative and innovative decisions.

You will learn to connect with your inner self and your source of inspiration.

By listening to your instincts and trusting your intuition, you will be able to unleash your creativity and turn your ideas into reality.

CHAPTER 18: LEARN TO FAIL

When you are willing to take risks to achieve your dreams, you face a big challenge: learning to fail.

Failure is something we all have at one time or another, but it's important to understand that failure is also an inevitable part of creativity and innovation.

It's an essential process to successfully achieving your goals.

To begin with, it is important to understand that failure is a natural and inevitable process.

It can happen at any point in the creative and innovative process.

It is impossible to predict all outcomes in advance and some things will not always work as planned.

That's why it's important to understand that failure is natural and inevitable and not to be discouraged by it.

It is also important to understand that failure is not an end in itself. In fact, failure can often be a means to progress.

For example, if you try a new product and it doesn't work, you can learn from your mistakes and find ways to make it more effective.

By taking the time to understand what went wrong and trying new approaches, you can find more effective ways to achieve your goal.

Finally, it's important to understand that failure can be a source of motivation and inspiration.

Sometimes, failures can be useful tools to boost your creativity and innovation.

When you fail, take time to reflect on what happened and try to find ways to be more successful next time.

When you use these failures as inspiration and motivation, you will be more willing to take risks and test new ideas.

In summary, learning to fail is an essential part of creativity and innovation.

It is a natural and inevitable process, but it can also be a source of motivation and inspiration.

By taking the time to analyze your failures and understand what went wrong, you can find more effective ways to achieve your goals.

Thus, by learning to fail, you can stimulate your creativity and unleash your creative potential.

CHAPTER 19: FINDING YOUR VOICE

One of the keys to unlocking your creativity and turning your ideas into reality is to find your voice.

Voice is a powerful tool for making sense of your ideas and communicating them consistently and effectively.

Your voice is what sets you apart from others and allows you to express yourself with conviction.

Without your voice, your ideas will not come across with the same strength and depth.

What is your voice?

It is a reflection of your personality and values.

It is the tone you use to communicate your ideas and the style that accompanies them, and it is the way you present your ideas and their implications.

It is what differentiates you from others and allows you to convey your message with greater impact.

Finding your voice can be intimidating and difficult.

However, once you find it, it becomes your strength and your guide.

Here are some tips to help you find your voice:

1. Find your identity.

Having a clear understanding of your identity is essential to finding your voice.

Who are you?

What makes you unique?

What do you want to say to the world?

Once you have a clear understanding of your identity, you can begin to define your voice and find the tone and style that defines you.

2. Listen to yourself.

Once you have a clear understanding of your identity, take time to listen to yourself.

Listen to your inner voice and explore what is important to you and what you want to share with others.

3. Be authentic.

Your voice is a reflection of your identity and values.

Be authentic and express clearly what you think and feel.

4. <u>Be creative.</u>

Use metaphors, analogies and images to express your ideas and emotions.

This can help add depth to your message and make it more powerful.

5. <u>Be brave.</u>

Speaking in your own voice can be intimidating.

However, speaking with courage and conviction is key to getting your ideas across.

6. <u>Be flexible.</u>

Your voice can change and adapt to different circumstances.

Don't be too rigid and be prepared to adapt to different situations and audiences.

7. <u>Practice.</u>

Practice is the key to finding your voice and becoming more comfortable with it.

Find opportunities to use your voice and practice regularly to feel more comfortable and confident.

Finding your voice is a process that can take time.

However, once you find it, it will become a powerful tool for expressing your ideas and emotions clearly and convincingly.

It is important to take the time to find your voice and use it with courage and conviction to unleash your creativity and turn your ideas into reality.

CHAPTER 20: MOVING TOWARDS ACHIEVEMENT

A project is useless if it remains in a dream state.

To encourage change, creativity and innovation, you need to move forward and take action.

Once the idea and plan are in place, it's time to start working.

This is what we call moving toward completion.

Moving toward completion involves taking the steps necessary to help you achieve the goals you've set.

It starts with planning and organizing your project. Take the time to analyze the plan and decide on the steps needed to execute it.

Identify the tasks to be accomplished, set a timetable and designate who will be responsible for each task.

Set realistic and measurable short-term goals and develop strategies to achieve them.

Once your project is planned and organized, it's time to take action.

The key here is to focus on the results, not the process.
Focus on what you need to do to achieve your goals.

Make changes and adjustments if necessary.

Use tools to help you stay organized and focused on your goals.

Achieving your goals also involves gathering the resources you need to reach your goals.

Identify the outside people or resources you need to complete your project.

Evaluate the costs and benefits of different options. Find partners and suppliers who can help you achieve your goals.

Finally, another important part of moving toward completion is to be flexible.

It is important to be willing to modify the plan if necessary and make changes as you move forward.

The best plans adapt to changing circumstances and conditions.

Plans are living and evolving.

Advancing toward completion can be an exciting adventure.

It's a way to take control of your project and turn it into a tangible reality.

It's about using your creativity, ingenuity and determination to achieve your goals.

If you want to encourage creativity and innovation, advancing to completion is a great way to do so.

<u>WHO IS JANE HAWKINS?</u>

Jane Hawkins is a prolific and passionate author who began writing at the age of 17.

She has published more than 100 books in a variety of genres, ranging from fiction to personal development.

She is known for her unique and interesting style, and her books are read by people all over the world.

Her passion for writing is what drives her every day and she writes in both French and English.

Her words are captivating and her stories are full of inspiration and emotion.

She loves to share her passion for literature with her readers, and offer them new perspectives.

If you have enjoyed a Jane Hawkins book, please leave her a positive review on Amazon!

<u>Notes :</u>

87

....
....
....
....
....
....
....
....
....
....
....
....
....
....
....
....
....
....
....
....
....
....